© Copyright 2021 - All rights reserved.

You may not reproduce, duplicate or send the contents of this book without direct written permission from the author. You cannot hereby despite any circumstance blame the publisher or hold him or her to legal responsibility for any reparation, compensations, or monetary forfeiture owing to the information included herein, either in a direct or an indirect way.

Legal Notice: This book has copyright protection. You can use the book for personal purpose. You should not sell, use, alter, distribute, quote, take excerpts or paraphrase in part or whole the material contained in this book without obtaining the permission of the author first.

Disclaimer Notice: You must take note that the information in this document is for casual reading and entertainment purposes only.
We have made every attempt to provide accurate, up to date and reliable information. We do not express or imply guarantees of any kind. The persons who read admit that the writer is not occupied in giving legal, financial, medical or other advice. We put this book content by sourcing various places.

Please consult a licensed professional before you try any techniques shown in this book. By going through this document, the book lover comes to an agreement that under no situation is the author accountable for any forfeiture, direct or indirect, which they may incur because of the use of material contained in this document, including, but not limited to, — errors, omissions, or inaccuracies.

Copyright© The Dancing Pages Publishing House
2020

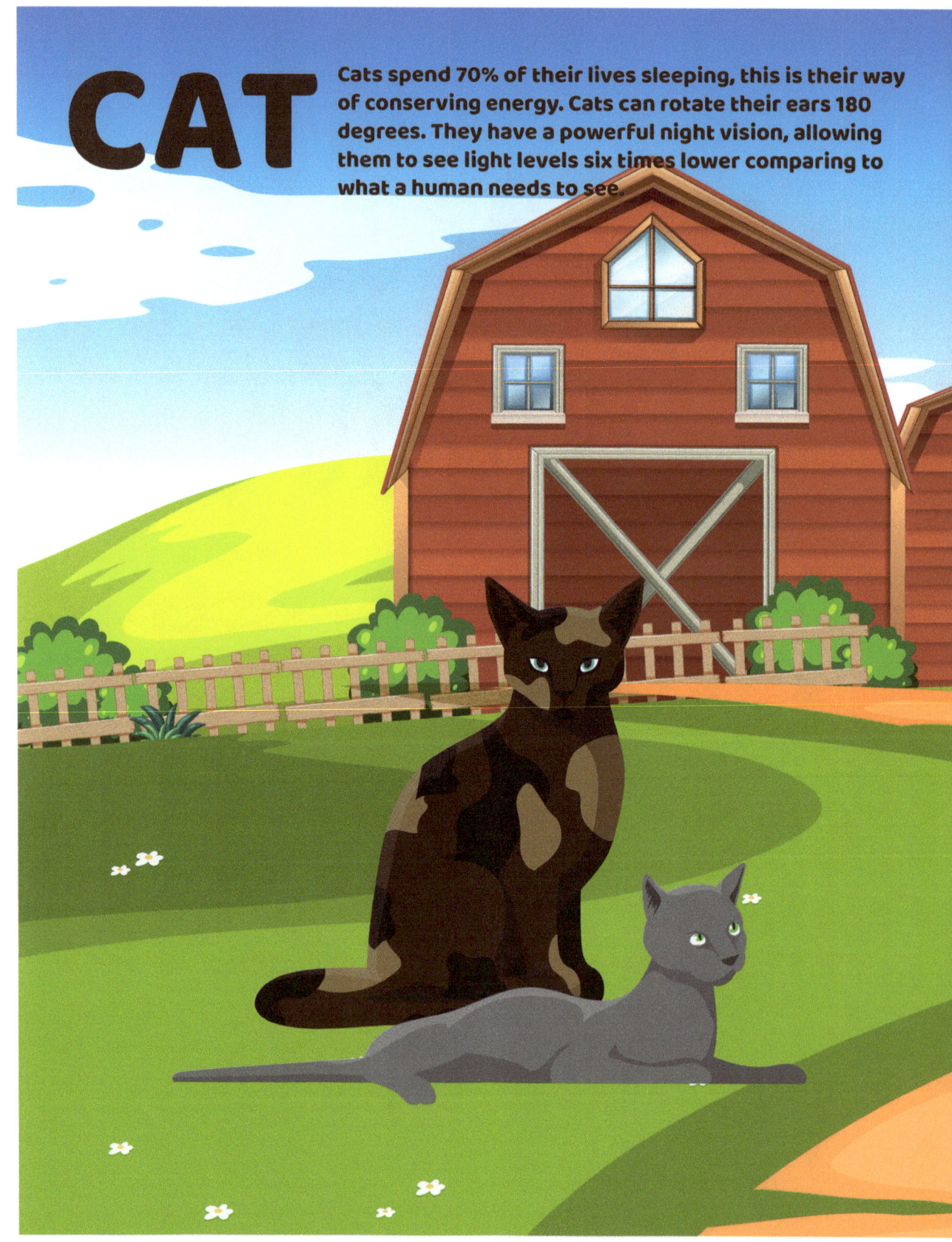

CAT

Cats spend 70% of their lives sleeping, this is their way of conserving energy. Cats can rotate their ears 180 degrees. They have a powerful night vision, allowing them to see light levels six times lower comparing to what a human needs to see.

DOG

It is a myth that dogs are color blind. They can actually see in color, it is similar to our vision at dusk. A dog's nose prints are as unique as a human's fingerprints and can be used to accurately identify them.

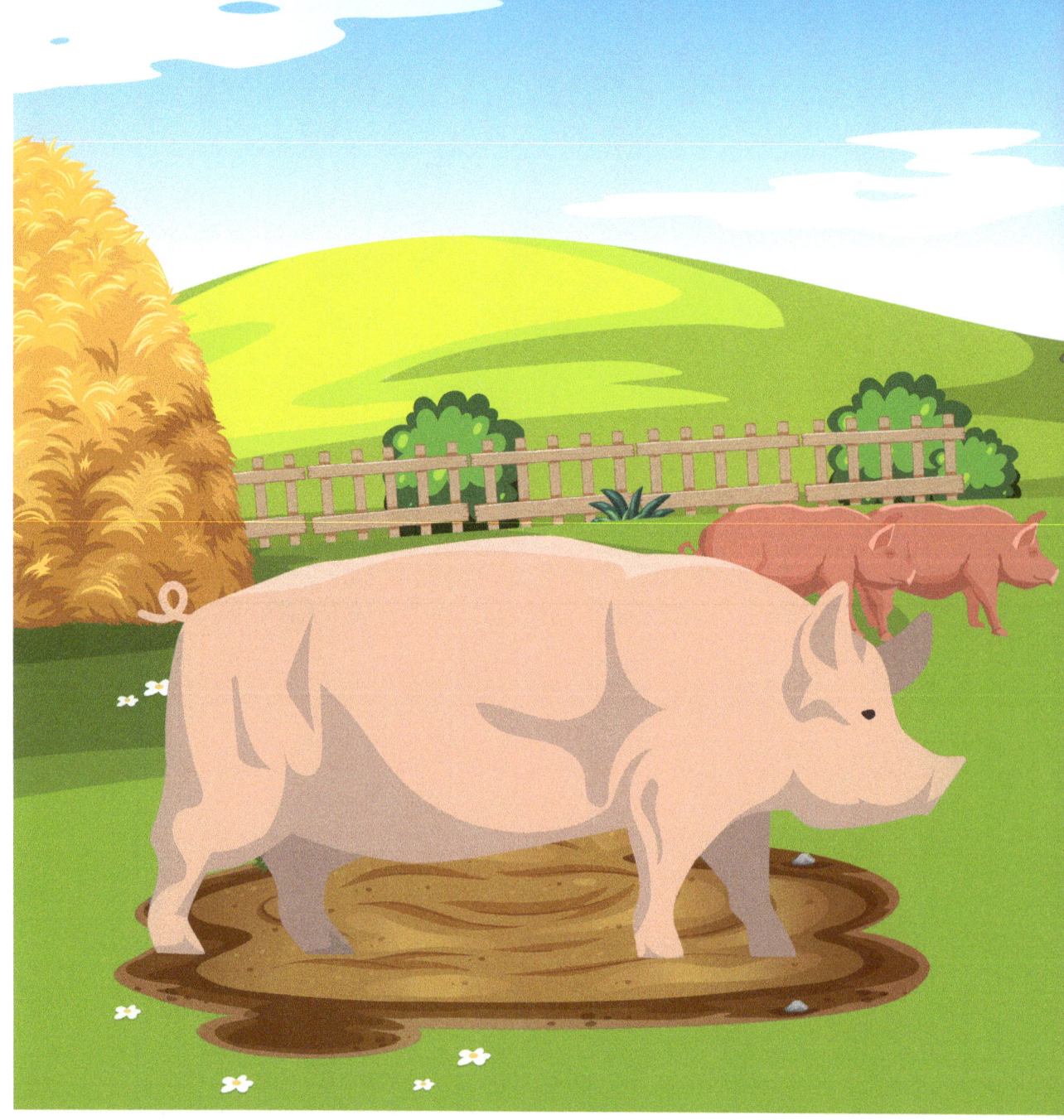

PIG

Pigs are smart! They have excellent memory as they can remember people and objects and recognize them after many years. They are playful animals, enjoy scratching themselves on trees, like to get massages, and relaxing while listening to music.

COW

A cow has 32 teeth, and will chew about 40-50 times a minute. They're always "vegetarian fed". Another interesting fact is that cows can see almost 360 degrees. As a result of this near-panoramic view, they can watch for predators from all angles.

Horse

Horses sleep standing up. They do it laying down too, but only for short periods of time. Because horse's eyes are on the side of their head they are capable of seeing nearly 360 degrees at one time.

RAM

Ram use plants and other substances that have no nutritional value for them, to prevent or treat disease, and teach their young to do the same.

SHEEP

Sheep are emotionally complex animals, they are capable of experiencing a wide range of emotions, just as humans do. Sheep can be pessimists and optimists!

ROOSTER

A very interesting fact about Roosters is that they can predict the weather with their cockcrowing. Also, sounds which we call the crowing and clucking are the language of communication. They seem to us to be the same, but these sounds have more than 30 options.

CHICKEN

Chickens are very intelligent birds. They are capable to know your house and your "friends". If you take the chicken out of the coop for a couple of days, and then return back, the tribesmen will remember her and will take back.

TURKEY

Turkeys are known to exhibit over 20 distinct vocalisations, including a distinctive gobble that is produced by males. Turkeys are intelligent and sensitive animals being highly social.

GOOSE

Geese are very loyal. They mate for life and are protective of their partners and offspring. Geese have impressive visual capabilities! The way their eyes are structured allows them to see things in much finer detail at a further distance than humans!

BULL

This is a myth that bulls got angry when seeing a red piece of clothing. Why? Because they are colour blind.

DONKEY

Donkeys have an incredible memory – they can recognise areas and other donkeys they were with up to 25 years ago. Also, Donkeys are very strong and intelligent. A donkey is stronger than a horse of the same size.

RABBIT

Rabbits are meticulously clean animals. Much like a dog, a pet rabbit can be taught to come to his/her name, sit in your lap, and do simple tricks. Another interesting fact is that their teeth never stop growing, but they never get too long because they're gradually worn down as the rabbit chews on grasses, wildflowers and vegetables.

MOUSE

Mice, much like other rodents, have teeth that never stop growing. Their teeth grow at a rate of 0.3mm a day! Also, they can squeeze through the tiniest gaps and are fantastic climbers.

PONY

Ponies are small horses, but they are much stronger than normal horses. Ponies are easy to look after, requiring half of the food a horse would ask if it was the same weight.

BUFFALO

Buffalos are amazing swimmers. They will swim through deep waters to find better grazing areas. They do not have a very good eyesight, but their hearing and especially their smell are exceptional.

DUCK

All ducks have waterproof feathers. Even when the duck dives deeply into the water, the downy underlayer of feathers right next to the skin will stay completely dry.

SPARROW

Sparrows are very sociable birds, often nesting in colonies. Sparrows are around 14-16 cm long. These little birds prefer being in close association to human settlements, including urban and rural areas. They inhabit on ideal sparrow habitat nesting on buildings, roofs, and houses.

DOVE

Doves or the peace birds are amazing! Their capacity to find the way home over hundreds, even thousands of kilometres is unrivalled in the animal kingdom. Also, Doves have been used as messengers for thousands of years, particularly during the wars.

THANK YOU.

We hope you enjoyed our book.
As a small family company, your feedback is very important to us.
Please let us know how you like our book at:

the.dancing.pages@gmail.com

www.ingramcontent.com/pod-product-compliance
Lightning Source LLC
LaVergne TN
LVHW070211080526
838202LV00063B/6587